I0007732

Google Gemini AI Crash Course in One Hour

Greg Lim

Copyright © 2024 Greg Lim
All rights reserved.

Copyright © 2024 by Greg Lim

All rights reserved.
No part of this book may be reproduced in any form or by any electronic or mechanical means including information storage and retrieval systems, without permission in writing from the author. The only exception is by a reviewer, who may quote short excerpts in a review.

First Edition: April 2024

Table of Contents

Preface

About this book

In this book, we take you on a fun, hands-on crash course to learning Google Gemini AI. You'll start building your first Gemini AI app within minutes. Every section is written in a bite-sized manner and straight to the point as I don't want to waste your time (and most certainly mine) on the content you don't need.

In the course of this book, we will cover:
- Chapter 1: Introduction to Gemini Pro
- Chapter 2: Generating Text from a Text Only Input
- Chapter 3: Generating Text from both Text and Image Inputs
- Chapter 4: Building a Multi-Turn Conversation Chatbot
- Chapter 5: Build a Conversational ChatBot

The goal of this book is to teach you Google Gemini AI in a manageable way without overwhelming you. We focus only on the essentials and cover the material in a hands-on practice manner for you to code along.

Getting Book Updates

To receive updated versions of the book, subscribe to our mailing list by sending a mail to support@i-ducate.com. I try to update my books to use the latest version of software, libraries and will update the codes/content in this book. So do subscribe to my list to receive updated copies!

Contact and Code Examples

Contact me at support@i-ducate.com to obtain the source files used in this book. Comments or questions concerning this book can also be directed to the same.

Chapter 1: Introduction to Gemini Pro

In this book, we will be learning how to use Google's AI model, Gemini Pro and build our own AI chatbot.

What is Gemini?

Gemini is a series of multimodal generative AI models developed by Google. Gemini models can accept text and image prompts, depending on the model variation you choose, and output text responses.

Much like in ChatGPT, if you go to Google Gemini (*gemini.google.com*), we can feed in a text prompt "What day of the week is it?" and receive a response like:

We can also feed in images as prompts. For eg., if I upload the below picture and ask, "What is in the photo?" we should receive a text response "This image is of a dog wearing sunglasses sitting on a beach".

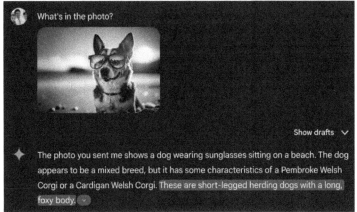

Furthermore, the conversation with Gemini considers the previous messages we sent as context. For eg. I ask "what does it like to eat":

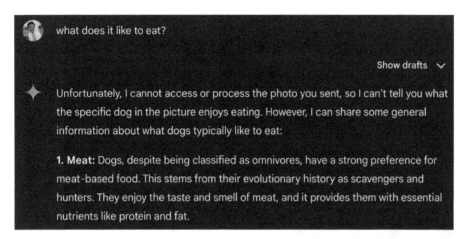

Because Gemini stores the chat history as context, it knows that 'it' is referring to the dog in the photo

We can leveraging Gemini to build our own apps by interacting with the Gemini API. The Gemini API allows us to perform exactly what the Gemini app UI allows us to do.

Go to the Gemini API documentation by going to *ai.google.dev* and selecting 'Read Gemini API docs':

You are brought to the documentation:

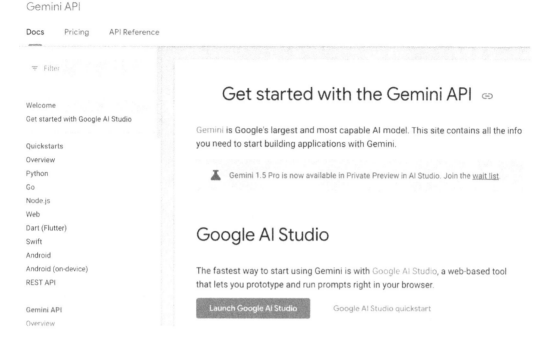

We will go into the good parts of the documentation later on.

To recap, Gemini is a series of multi modal generative AI models developed by Google that you can interact with via an API or via the Gemini app.

Getting our API Key to Work with Gemini

Now let's focus on getting our API key operational with Gemini. It's crucial to keep your API key confidential and not to share it. If your API key is compromised, it could be used by others in their projects, incurring significant charges.

This caution extends to exposing your key in any client-side code, meaning in an application built without a backend and published online. In such cases, the code can be easily inspected and the API key extracted for unauthorized use.

To securely utilize your API key, ensure that requests are channeled through your own backend server, where the API key can be securely stored as an environment variable or within a key management service. We will illustrate how to do this in the course of this book.

Let's proceed to obtain our API key. Go to *ai.google.dev*.

Note: You might be required to sign in, or if you are already signed in using Google Chrome, you could just go ahead.

Select 'Get Gemini API key in Google AI studio'.

You will be brought to Google AI Studio where you can enter prompts, such as "In what year did the Titanic sank?" and then press enter for the chat to respond '1912'.

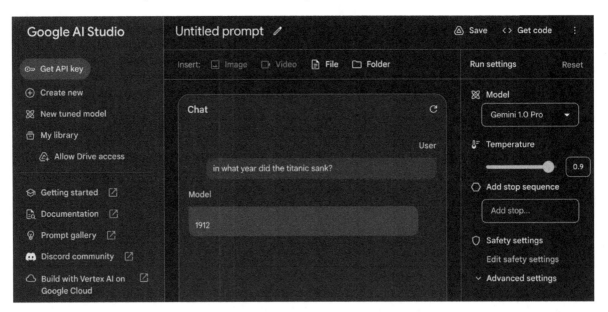

Additionally, you have the option to select the model from a dropdown menu:

and adjust the temperature setting:

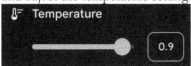

Temperature influences the creativity of our model:
- higher temperature results in more creativity
- lower temperature: results in more factual and objective outputs which reduce potential inaccuracies or hallucinations from the model.

You should select an appropriate temperature depending on the nature of the application. For apps that generate article titles or children's fiction stories, a higher temperature is preferred for more creativity. But for summarizing a legal document or a health report, we need more factual outputs, and thus, a lower temperature is more suitable.

Now, to obtain your API key, on the left, select 'Get API Key':

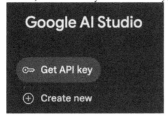

Go ahead and select 'Create API key'.

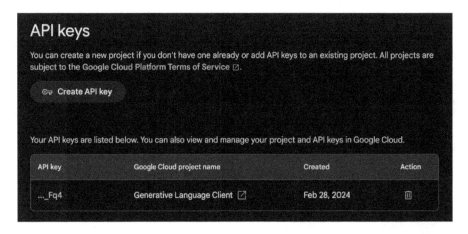

Copy the key and keep it safe. Do not share it or put it in any code that can be visible to anyone.

You can delete API keys and create new ones if you want. For example, if one is compromised, be sure to delete it quickly.

Models

We can get access to the Gemini generative AI models and their methods through the Gemini API. The popular ones are:

- **Generate text from text-only input** by using the *gemini-pro* model with the *generateContent* method to generate text output.
- **Generate text from text-and-image input** (multimodal) with the *gemini-pro-vision* model with the *generateContent* method to generate text output:
- **Build multi-turn conversations (chat)** using the *gemini-pro* model. The state of conversations are managed by for you, so you don't have to store the conversation history yourself.

We will look at how these work. In this book, we will be using Node.js. So make sure to have Node.js version 18 or above installed, along with *npm*.

In the Terminal, select a location and create a folder (used to store our files later). I create and name my folder 'geminipad' with:

```
mkdir geminipad
```

Change directory to the folder and initialize the project by running:

```
cd geminipad
npm init
```

You will asked a series of questions, eg. package name, version, description, entry point, and so on. Just proceed with the default values by leaving the fields blank and selecting 'enter'.

This will create an initial *package.json* file in the folder.

In your preferred code editor (in this book, I will be using VS Code), open the folder. It should look something like:

```
EXPLORER                    {} package.json ×

∨ GEM...  ⬚  ⬚  ↻  ⊟        {} package.json > ...
  {} package.json            1   {
                             2       "name": "geminipad",
                             3       "version": "1.0.0",
                             4       "description": "",
                             5       "main": "index.js",
                                 ▷ Debug
                             6       "scripts": {
                             7         "test": "echo \"Error: no test specified\" && exit 1"
                             8       },
                             9       "author": "",
                            10       "license": "ISC"
                            11   }
                            12
```

Now, let's proceed to install the required *generative-ai* dependency.

In the Terminal, run:

```
npm install @google/generative-ai
```

Start Script

Next, we will install nodemon to automatically detect and respond to changes in source files. Install the nodemon package with:

```
npm i nodemon
```

Let's proceed to create our index.js file now.

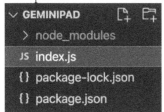

We can then run:

```
nodemon index.js
```

This will initiate monitoring of the index.js file for changes.

Initialize the Generative Model

Now, we'll initialize the generative model by adding the below into index.js:

```
const { GoogleGenerativeAI } = require("@google/generative-ai");
```

We declare a constant GoogleGenerativeAI and import the Google Generative AI module.

Getting the Gemini API Key

After importing the Google Generative AI module, we'll need to include the API key. To be extra cautious and not expose the API key, we create an .env file for storing such secrets. Create the *.env* file with the following:

```
API_KEY=AIzaSyA2q3uOBIJoCSnvWJ1Vh7DM6tMJv7a_Fq4
```

We assign our API key to the variable API_KEY (you should of course pass in your own API key).

Now in index.js, we can access our API key by adding in bold:

```
const { GoogleGenerativeAI } = require("@google/generative-ai");
require('dotenv').config()
const genAI = new GoogleGenerativeAI(process.env.API_KEY);
```

However, we do need the *dotenv* package for this. Install it by running:

```
npm i dotenv
```

After initializing the generative model, we have access to its methods and properties, which are now available under the *genAI* variable. For instance, we can call the *getGenerativeModel* method to select a specific model. Add the following in bold:

```
const { GoogleGenerativeAI } = require("@google/generative-ai");
require('dotenv').config()
const genAI = new GoogleGenerativeAI(process.env.API_KEY);

const model = genAI.getGenerativeModel({model: "gemini-pro"})
```

14

We choose the 'Gemini Pro' model for this example.

If you need to use a different model, change the string accordingly eg.to use 'Gemini Pro Vision' we change the text:

```
const model = genAI.getGenerativeModel({model: "gemini-pro-version"})
```

To ensure this works, we can console log out the model:

index.js

```
const { GoogleGenerativeAI } = require("@google/generative-ai");
require('dotenv').config()
const genAI = new GoogleGenerativeAI(process.env.API_KEY);
const model = genAI.getGenerativeModel({model: "gemini-pro-version"})
```

console.log(model)

And in the Terminal (remember to run *nodemon index.js*), we get something like:

```
GenerativeModel {
  apiKey: 'AIzaSyA2q3uOBIJoCSnvWJ1Vh7DM6tMJv7a_Fq4',
  model: 'models/gemini-pro-version',
  generationConfig: {},
  safetySettings: [],
  requestOptions: {}
}
```

Great, everything appears to be working well.

Chapter 2: Generating Text from a Text Only Input

Now, let's proceed to the task of generating text from a text-only input. i.e. when our input prompt consists solely of text, we expect the model to return a text response.

To achieve this, we will use the 'Gemini Pro' model and its *generateText* method.

In the existing index.js file, write a function for generating the text. Add the following in **bold**:

```
const { GoogleGenerativeAI } = require("@google/generative-ai");
require('dotenv').config()
const genAI = new GoogleGenerativeAI(process.env.API_KEY);
const model = genAI.getGenerativeModel({model: "gemini-pro"})

async function run() {
  const prompt = "Write me an article about investing."
  const result = await model.generateContent(prompt)
  const response = await result.response
  const text = response.text()
  console.log(text);
}
```

Code Explanation

```
async function run() {
  const prompt = "Write me an article about investing."
```

We added an asynchronous function named *run*. In it, we define our prompt "Write me an article about investing.".

```
  const result = await model.generateContent(prompt)
```

We retrieve the result by sending this prompt to the *generateContent* method of the 'Gemini Pro' model.

```
  const response = await result.response
  const text = response.text()
  console.log(text);
```

We capture the model's response, which is also an asynchronous operation, so we'll await this response and store it in a variable named *response*. From there, we can extract the text and assign it to a variable called *text*.

Finally, let's output this text with a console log to observe the result of our function.

Running our function

We then run our function by adding in **bold**:

```
const { GoogleGenerativeAI } = require("@google/generative-ai");
  ..

async function run() {
  ...
}
```

run();

And then hit save. And we should get something like:

Unlocking the World of Investing: A Comprehensive Guide

Investing is an essential part of financial planning, allowing individuals to grow their wealth over time and secure their financial future. However, navigating the world of investing can be daunting, especially for beginners. This article provides a comprehensive guide to help you understand the basics of investing and empower you to make informed investment decisions.

Understanding the Basics
...
...
...
Conclusion

Investing is a powerful tool that can help you grow your wealth and secure your financial ...

We prompted it with "**Write me an article about investing."** and indeed, it produced an article about investing.

The outcome looks great. And keep in mind the code we've demonstrated is to generate text responses from text prompts.

Now, let's next look at generating text from both text and image inputs.

Chapter 3: Generating Text from both Text and Image Inputs

Now let's explore generating text from both text and image inputs. This is referred to as multimodal input. Gemini offers a multimodal model known as Gemini Pro Vision (not to be confused with Gemini Pro). This model allows us to input both text and images to generate text.

Let's proceed with a simple example to demonstrate how you can expand upon this in our Node.js application. We'll be using the Gemini Pro Vision model, specifically the *generateContent* method, to process both text and image inputs.

To begin, let's return to where we left off in index.js.

First, update the model to use the Gemini Pro Vision model by adding in **bold**:

```
const { GoogleGenerativeAI } = require("@google/generative-ai");
require('dotenv').config()
const genAI = new GoogleGenerativeAI(process.env.API_KEY);
const model = genAI.getGenerativeModel({model: "gemini-pro-vision"})
```

Now we need to include an additional package that helps us handle image files more effectively. This package is called 'fs', short for file system. Add in **bold**:

```
const { GoogleGenerativeAI } = require("@google/generative-ai");
require('dotenv').config()
const fs = require('fs')
...
```

We next need to install *fs* with:

```
npm i fs
```

Now we're going to have to convert local file information to a GoogleGenerativeAI.part object. To do this, we write a function *fileToGenerativePart*:

```
function fileToGenerativePart(path, mimeType) {
  return {
    inlineData: {
      data: Buffer.from(fs.readFileSync(path)).toString("base64"),
      mimeType
    },
  };
```

```
}
```

Code Explanation

```
function fileToGenerativePart(path, mimeType) {
```

We provide two parameters to the function: a file path and a MIME type.

```
  return {
    inlineData: {
      data: Buffer.from(fs.readFileSync(path)).toString("base64"),
      mimeType
    },
  };
```

The function returns an object containing a 'data' property, which is itself an object.

```
      data: Buffer.from(fs.readFileSync(path)).toString("base64"),
      mimeType
```

This 'data' object includes the file data, which we'll read from the file system using fs.readFileSync and then convert to a base64-encoded string.

We also include the MIME type to enable us to create a buffer for our file's data.

run()

Let's proceed by writing our asynchronous function that will execute this process.

We'll define an async function run by adding in the below code:

```
async function run() {
    const prompt = "What's different between these pictures?";
}
```

Inside this function, we set our prompt asking, 'What's different between these pictures?'. As you might guess, in this example, we will upload two image files and ask Gemini to tell us the difference.

So pick any two image files you want to compare. For me, I will use the below two images:

(at point of writing this book, Taylor Swift is having a concert in my country at the Singapore National Stadium – right pic)

Drag and drop your image files on the same level as index.js. I've named mine simply image1.png and image2.png.

Next, we'll retrieve our image data using the *fileToGenerativePart* function we defined earlier. Add in **bold**:

```
async function run() {
    const prompt = "What's different between these pictures?";

    const imageParts = [
      fileToGenerativePart("image1.png", "image/png"),
      fileToGenerativePart("image2.png", "image/png"),
    ];

    const result = await model.generateContent([prompt, ...imageParts]);
    const response = await result.response;
    const text = response.text();
    console.log(text);
  }

  run();
```

Code Explanation

```
const imageParts = [
  fileToGenerativePart("image1.png", "image/png"),
  fileToGenerativePart("image2.png", "image/png"),
];
```

We'll have two image paths, and we apply the *fileToGenerativePart* function to both. If your image file is jpeg, you will do something like: *fileToGenerativePart("image2.jpeg", "image/jpeg")*

```
const result = await model.generateContent([prompt, ...imageParts]);
```

We then call *generateContent* and pass in the prompt and *imageParts* array in.

```
const response = await result.response;
const text = response.text();
console.log(text);
```

We then await to get the response, get the text and console log the text.

```
run();
```

Now let's run it.

And we get the following response:

The first picture is a picture of Taylor Swift performing on stage. She is wearing a sparkly bodysuit and is surrounded by pink lights. The second picture is a picture of the Singapore National Stadium. It is a large, white dome-shaped stadium that is located in Singapore.

Extremely accurate! This is how you would use the *generateContent* method from Gemini Pro Vision.

This is the entire file:

```
const { GoogleGenerativeAI } = require("@google/generative-ai");
require('dotenv').config()
const fs = require('fs')
const genAI = new GoogleGenerativeAI(process.env.API_KEY);
const model = genAI.getGenerativeModel({model: "gemini-pro-vision"})

function fileToGenerativePart(path, mimeType) {
    return {
      inlineData: {
        data: Buffer.from(fs.readFileSync(path)).toString("base64"),
        mimeType
      },
    };
  }

async function run() {
    const prompt = "What's different between these pictures?";

    const imageParts = [
        fileToGenerativePart("image1.png", "image/png"),
        fileToGenerativePart("image2.png", "image/png"),
    ];

    const result = await model.generateContent([prompt, ...imageParts]);
    const response = await result.response;
    const text = response.text();
    console.log(text);
}

run();
```

Next, let's look at building a multi-turn conversation chatbot.

Chapter 4: Building a Multi-Turn Conversation Chatbot

Using the Gemini Pro model, we can create chatbots that take the history of your multi turn conversation (like a chat) as context for your next question.

Let's proceed with this. In our existing index.js code, we are going to switch the model to Gemini Pro. We also don't need the file system at the moment. So make the changes in **bold**:

```
const { GoogleGenerativeAI } = require("@google/generative-ai");
require('dotenv').config()
const fs = require('fs')
const genAI = new GoogleGenerativeAI(process.env.API_KEY);
const model = genAI.getGenerativeModel({model: "gemini-pro-vision"})
```

We can also remove the *fileToGenerativePart* function for now.

Let's go ahead and write our function. We will create an asynchronous function called *run* with the below code:

```
async function run() {
  const chat = model.startChat({
    history: [
      {
        role: "user",
        parts: [{text:"Hello, I have 2 dogs in my house."}],
      },
      {
        role: "model",
        parts: [{text:"Great to meet you. What would you like to
know?"}],
      },
    ],
    generationConfig: {
      maxOutputTokens: 100,
    },
  });

  const msg = "How many paws are in my house?";

  const result = await chat.sendMessage(msg);
  const response = await result.response;
  const text = response.text();
```

```
    console.log(text);
}

run();
```

Code Explanation

```
const chat = model.startChat({
    history: [
        ...
    ],
    generationConfig: {
        ...
    },
});
```

We initiate the chat process by using the *startChat* method of the model and passing an object to it. The result is stored in a constant named *chat*.

Within chat, we have a *history* array with the *user* role and the *model* role. The *user* role provides the prompt, eg. "Hello, I have 2 dogs in my house."

```
        history: [
          {
            role: "user",
            parts: [{text:"Hello, I have 2 dogs in my house."}],
          },
```

The *model* role provides the responses. It responds with "Great to meet you. What would you like to know?"

```
          {
            role: "model",
            parts: [{text:"Great to meet you. What would you like to
know?"}],
          },
```

We then use *sendMessage* to send a new user message. We want to ask a follow up question of "how many paws are in my house":

```
  const msg = "How many paws are in my house?";

  const result = await chat.sendMessage(msg);
      ...
```

So we've got the history, and also the new question we want to ask.

We proceed to obtain the result with *sendMessage* which appends both the new message and the response to the chat history.

```
const response = await result.response;
const text = response.text();
console.log(text);
```

After we await the response from the result, we extract the text from it and console.log it.

Running our App

Now let's run this function by adding:

```
run()
```

And in the Terminal, we should get a response like:

*If you have 2 dogs in your house, and each dog has 4 paws, then there are a total of 2 * 4 = 8 paws in your house.*

Great! We'll be using this approach to build our own chatbot for the upcoming final project.

In case you need the complete code of index.js:

```
const { GoogleGenerativeAI } = require("@google/generative-ai");
require('dotenv').config()

const genAI = new GoogleGenerativeAI(process.env.API_KEY);
const model = genAI.getGenerativeModel({model: "gemini-pro"})

async function run() {
    const chat = model.startChat({
        history: [
            {
              role: "user",
              parts: [{text:"Hello, I have 2 dogs in my house."}],
            },
            {
              role: "model",
              parts: [{text:"Great to meet you. What would you like to
know?"}],
            },
        ],
        generationConfig: {
```

```
        maxOutputTokens: 100,
      },
    });

    const msg = "How many paws are in my house?";

    const result = await chat.sendMessage(msg);
    const response = await result.response;
    const text = response.text();
    console.log(text);
}

run();
```

Chapter 5: Build a Conversational ChatBot

Let's now build our chatbot. In a new folder, let's first create the frontend for our project using React by running:

```
npx create-react-app <project_name>
```

ie. `npx create-react-app geminichatbot`

This will create a react app folder with all the pre-configured files for us.
Note: this chapter assumes some basic knowledge of React. If React is something new to you and you want a crash course, contact support@i-ducate.com for a copy of my React book.

As what we have done previously, go to *ai.google.dev* and get your API key from the Google AI Studio.

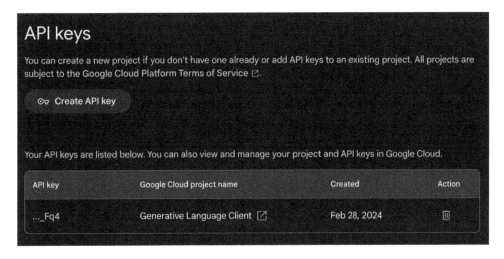

In your code editor (I am using VS Code), open the folder that *create-react-app* created for us:

You will see the 'src' directory, a package.json file, and all the dependencies in *node_modules* we will use.

First, we will simplify things a bit by doing some cleaning up. In the /src, we delete a couple of files that we won't be using eg. setupTests.js, pp.test.js, index.css, app.css, 'reportWebVitals'.

So our index.js will look like:
```
import React from 'react';
import ReactDOM from 'react-dom/client';
import App from './App';

const root = ReactDOM.createRoot(document.getElementById('root'));
root.render(
  <React.StrictMode>
    <App />
  </React.StrictMode>
);
```

And the files we will have left:

We won't be digging into CSS because we will use React Bootstrap so we can focus on the Google Gemini essentials.

The main files we will be working with are App.js and index.js.

Storing our Secret Key

Let's store our secret key. Like before, in the project folder, create a *.env* file to hold our API key.

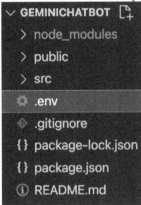

*Note: the .env file should be in the root project folder, not in 'src' or any other sub folder.

We'll store our Google Generative AI key in *.env* similar to what we have done before:

Remember to replace with your own API key.

Next, let's build out a simple front end using React Bootstrap. Refer to *react-bootstrap.netlify.app* for more information on React Bootstrap.

Installation

The best way to consume React-Bootstrap is via the npm package which you can install with `npm` (or `yarn` if you prefer).

If you plan on customizing the Bootstrap Sass files, or don't want to use a CDN for the stylesheet, it may be helpful to install vanilla Bootstrap as well.

```
npm install react-bootstrap bootstrap
```

Install React-Bootstap by running in the Terminal (in the project folder):

```
npm install react-bootstrap bootstrap
```

Next, include at the top of App.js:
```
import 'bootstrap/dist/css/bootstrap.min.css';
```

In App.js, we add a input control for the user to enter their message and also two buttons, 'Ask Me' and 'Clear'. Add the following into App.js:

```
import 'bootstrap/dist/css/bootstrap.min.css';
import Container from 'react-bootstrap/Container';
import Button from 'react-bootstrap/Button';
import Form from 'react-bootstrap/Form';

function App() {
  return (
    <Container>
        <Form.Control type="text" placeholder="Can you tell me about..."
        />
        <Button variant="primary" type="submit">
          Ask Me
        </Button>
        <Button variant="secondary" type="submit">
          Clear
        </Button>
    </Container>
  );
}

export default App;
```

Running our Frontend

To run our frontend, go to the Terminal, and in the project folder, run:

```
npm run start
```

And you should see your frontend running in the browser (localhost:3000):

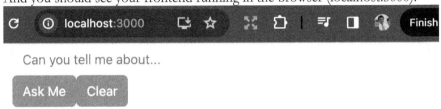

Implementing our Backend

Now that we have our frontend running, in the same folder, we will have our backend script called server.js.

Let's first install nodemon with:
```
npm i nodemon
```

(it will be useful to open up a separate Terminal to do so while the frontend is running)

Nodemon will listen to changes on the server.js file, which we will create next.

Go ahead and create server.js.

Note that server.js should be in root of the project directory (like .env), not in 'src'.

Let's run our backend with:

```
nodemon server.js
```

And we should see in the Terminal:

```
(base) MacBook-Air-2:geminichatbot user$ nodemon server.js
[nodemon] 2.0.12
[nodemon] to restart at any time, enter `rs`
[nodemon] watching path(s): *.*
[nodemon] watching extensions: js,mjs,json
[nodemon] starting `node server.js`
[nodemon] clean exit - waiting for changes before restart
```

Back to our Frontend

To handle and display errors met during the connection to Gemini, we create a 'error' state.

Let's start by importing and using *useState* from React in App.js by adding in **bold**:

```
import 'bootstrap/dist/css/bootstrap.min.css';
...
```

34

```
import {useState} from 'react';
...

function App() {
  const [error, setError] = useState("")
    ...
```

We set the initial value of *error* to an empty string "". *error* will hold the error message. To update it, we'll use *setError*. If there's an error—we should be able to detect and display it. Let's do that by adding in **bold**:

```
...
import Alert from 'react-bootstrap/Alert';

function App() {
  const [error, setError] = useState("")

  return (
    <Container>
        <Form.Control type="text" placeholder="Can you tell me about..."
        />
        <Button variant="primary" type="submit">
          Ask Me
        </Button>
        <Button variant="secondary" type="submit">
          Clear
        </Button>
        {error &&
          <Alert key="danger" variant="danger">
            {error}
          </Alert>
        }
    </Container>
  );
}

export default App;
```

Code Explanation

```
        {error &&
          <Alert key="danger" variant="danger">
            {error}
          </Alert>
        }
```

If an error exists, we will display a Alert component that shows the error. Otherwise, it won't be displayed. Eg.

Can you tell me about...

Ask Me   Clear

sample error

Value and ChatHistory States

We will next create our *value* (used to capture user input) and *chatHistory* states. In App.js, add:

```
function App() {
  const [error, setError] = useState("")
  const [value, setValue] = useState("")
  const [chatHistory, setChatHistory] = useState([])
  ...
```

chatHistory is initialized to be an empty array.

Let's link *value* to our input control. Handle the *onChange* event to update the value based on what's typed into the input by adding in **bold**:

```
function App() {
  ...

  return (
    <Container>
      <Form.Control type="text" placeholder="Can you tell me about..."
        value={value}
        onChange={(e) => setValue(e.target.value)}
      />
      <Button variant="primary" type="submit">
        Ask Me
      </Button>
      ...
```

We create a function that captures the event (denoted as *e*) and then sets the value using *setValue(e.target.value)*.

Sending our Values to our API

To send our user entered values to our API, we write a function *getResponse*, which receives the response from the API. In App.js, add in bold:

```
function App() {
  ...
  const [chatHistory, setChatHistory] = useState([])

  const getResponse = async() => {
    if (!value){
      setError("Please ask a question.")
      return
    }
  }

  return (
    <Container>
        <Form.Control type="text" placeholder="Can you tell me about..."
          value={value}
          onChange={(e) => setValue(e.target.value)}
        />
        <Button variant="primary" type="submit" onClick={getResponse}>
          Ask Me
        </Button>
        ...
```

If the user didn't enter anything and clicks 'Ask Me', we want an error to show "Please ask a question." We do this by attaching the *getResponse* function to the *onClick* of the 'Ask Me' button.

So now, in the frontend, if you click on 'Ask Me', you get an error:

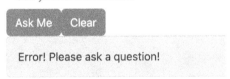

Try Catch to Handle Errors

Let's now employ try and catch blocks to handle errors. We'll try to execute some code in the *try* block.

If it fails, we'll catch any errors and log them to the console with *console.error(error)* and also set the *error* state.

Add in *getResponse*:

```
const getResponse = async() => {
  if (!value){
    setError("Error! Please ask a question!")
    return
  }

  try{

  }
  catch(error){
    console.error(error)
    setError(error)
  }
}
```

Sending our Data to the Backend

Options

Now, let's talk about what we're going to send to the backend. We add our *options* first. In *getResponse*, add:

```
const getResponse = async() => {
  ...

  try{
    const options = {
      method: 'POST',
      body: JSON.stringify({
        history: chatHistory,
        message: value
      }),
      headers:{
        'Content-Type':'application/json'
      }
    }
  }
  catch(error){
    ...
```

We'll be using the POST method for this operation. We send over an object which includes the entire chat history of previous questions ie. *chatHistory* and also the message which holds the latest text typed by the user. We use JSON.stringify to handle this.

We also set our headers where we choose content type JSON.

Response

We get the response from using await fetch, with the backend endpoint localhost:8000/gemini, and we send the options with it. Add in **bold**:

```
try{
  const options = {
  ...
  }
  const response = await
fetch('http://localhost:8000/gemini',options)
  const data = await response.text()
  console.log(data)
}
catch(error){
  console.error(error)
  setError(error)
}
```

Once the response comes back to us, we get text from it with *await response.text()*. We then console log the data to see what's coming back.

Backend

Let's now focus on our backend development. In **server.js**, we're going to specify port 8000 and also import several packages. Add in the code:

```
const PORT = 8000
const express = require('express')
const cors = require('cors')
const {GoogleGenerativeAI} = require("@google/generative-ai")
require('dotenv').config()
```

We'll install Express to aid in handling routing. Additionally, we'll instal CORS (Cross-Origin Resource Sharing) to address and prevent the common issue of blocked CORS requests when transmitting data from the frontend to the backend. The dotenv package will be utilized for securely storing secrets in our *.env* file, as demonstrated earlier.

Lastly, we require Google Generative AI. So in the Terminal, run:

```
npm i express cors dotenv @google/generative-ai
```

Next we add in **bold**:

```
const PORT = 8000
const express = require('express')
const cors = require('cors')
const {GoogleGenerativeAI} = require("@google/generative-ai")
require('dotenv').config()
const app = express()
app.use(cors())
app.use(express.json())
```

express() provides access to methods and properties that come with Express, and we save it to the const *app*.

We can now use app to get any method, so for example, *app.use(cors())*.

Because we are going to also pass JSON from the front end, we need to use *app.use(express.json())*

Next, we use Google Generative AI and pass in the API key. Add in **bold**:

```
...
const app = express()
app.use(cors())
app.use(express.json())

const genAI = new GoogleGenerativeAI(process.env.API_KEY);
```

We then listen on our PORT by adding:

```
app.listen(PORT, () => console.log(`listening on port ${PORT}`))
```

We pass the port as the first parameter to *app.listen* and as the second parameter, a callback function which console logs "listening on port 'port number'".

We can test run our backend by running:
```
nodemon server.js
```

and you should get something like:

```
[nodemon] starting `node server.js`
listening on port 8000
```

Creating our Route

Let's now proceed to define our route by adding the below in server.js:

```
...

...

...
app.listen(PORT, () => console.log(`listening on port ${PORT}`))

app.post('/gemini', async (req, res) => {
    console.log(req.body.history)
    console.log(req.body.message)
})
```

Code Explanation

We create a POST request route handler for the endpoint "gemini," as previously indicated in our frontend (App.js):

```
const response = await fetch('http://localhost:8000/gemini',options)
```

To retrieve the body of the request data from the frontend, we use req.body. We can extract the history and message of the body using: *req.body.history* and *req.body.message*.

Remember that back in our frontend (App.js), we specified the properties history and message:

```
const options = {
  method: 'POST',
  body: JSON.stringify({
    history: chatHistory,
    message: value
  }),
  ....
}
```

We log them to the console so its clearer what we are receiving from the frontend.

```
console.log(req.body.history)
console.log(req.body.message)
```

Let's try running our app. **Ensure both frontend and backend are running.** In my frontend, I will say:

> tell me about the declaration of independence

Ask Me   Clear

Click 'Ask Me' and in our backend, we can see in the Terminal:

```
[nodemon] restarting due to changes...
[nodemon] starting `node server.js`
listening on port 8000
[]
tell me about the declaration of independence
```

Note the two pieces of information being logged:
- *history*, which is currently an empty array [], and
- *value*, "tell me about the declaration of independence".

Sending *history* and *value* to Gemini Pro API

Next, we will proceed to send this data to the Gemini API. We specify the model:

```
app.post('/gemini', async (req, res) => {
    console.log(req.body.history)
    console.log(req.body.message)

    const model = genAI.getGenerativeModel({model:'gemini-pro'})
})
```

Next, let's set up the chat. We use the model and call its *startChat* method by adding the code in **bold**:

```
app.post('/gemini', async (req, res) => {
    ...
    const model = genAI.getGenerativeModel({model:'gemini-pro'})
    const chat = model.startChat({
        history: req.body.history
    })

    const msg = req.body.message
    const result = await chat.sendMessage(msg)
})
```

We pass in an object which includes the history available from *req.body.history*. We get the message from *req.body.message*. And we send the message to the chat with *await chat.sendMessage(msg)*.

The message, with the history, will be sent to the API. We then receive the result and the response from this operation by adding in **bold**:

```
app.post('/gemini', async (req, res) => {
    ...
    const msg = req.body.message
    const result = await chat.sendMessage(msg)

    const response = await result.response
    const text = response.text()

    console.log(text)
    res.send(text)
})
```

Given that *result.response* is asynchronous, we use await to pause execution until the operation completes and assign the result to a variable named *response*.

Following that, we extract the text from the response with *response.text()*.

Subsequently, we use *res.send(text)* to forward this text back to our frontend.

Receiving the Response on the Frontend

Once we receive the response on the frontend, we are currently logging it to the console (code in **bold**):

App.js

```
function App() {
    ...
  const getResponse = async() => {
    ...
    try{
      const options = {
      ...
      }
      const response = await
fetch('http://localhost:8000/gemini',options)
      const data = await response.text()
      console.log(data)
    }
```

```
catch(error){
   ...
}
}
```

We need to update the chat history with the latest response. Fill in the codes in **bold**:

```
try{
   ...
   const response = await
fetch('http://localhost:8000/gemini',options)
   const data = await response.text()
   console.log(data)
   setChatHistory(oldChatHistory => [...oldChatHistory, {
     role:"user",
     parts:[{text:value}]
   },
     {
       role: "model",
       parts:[{text:data}]
     }
   ])
   setValue("")
}
   ...
```

Code Explanation

setChatHistory(oldChatHistory => [...oldChatHistory, {...

We use *setChatHistory* to update *chatHistory* state. When dealing with arrays, it's crucial to first spread the existing state (*oldChatHistory*) into the array to maintain previous states.

```
{
  role:"user",
  parts:[{text:value}]
},
  {
    role: "model",
    parts:[{text:data}]
  }
```

We construct an object that aligns with the existing data structure defined by Google for chats ie. a user object representing the user who posed the question (*value*) and another object where the role is "model", with the response.

```
setValue("")
```

Finally, we set value back to empty string for the user to enter the next chat message.

Rendering on the Page

With the chat history updated, let's proceed to render it on the page. We will access the chat history and utilize the *map* function to iterate over each entry, rendering them within a designated div container (we will beautify the look later). Add the code in **bold**:

```
function App() {
    ...

    try{...
    }
    catch(error){...
    }
}

  return (
    <Container>
      ...
      ...
        {error &&
          <Alert key="danger" variant="danger">
            {error}
          </Alert>
        }
        <div>
          {chatHistory.map((chatItem, _index) =>
            <div key={_index}>
                <p>{chatItem.role}</p>
                <p>{chatItem.parts[0].text}</p>
            </div>)}
        </div>
    </Container>
  );
}
```

For each iteration, we map through *chatHistory*, taking into account both *chatItem* and its _index in the array. The index is passed as a key, though it's primarily used for React's internal tracking and not for any functional purpose in our application.

For each *chatItem*, we extract and display its role—identifying whether it was sent by the user or generated by the model. Additionally, we retrieve and display the corresponding text from each chat item.

```
{chatHistory.map((chatItem, _index) =>
  <div key={_index}>
      <p>{chatItem.role}</p>
      <p>{chatItem.parts[0].text}</p>
  </div>)}
```

Note: you have to console log and observe what the data structure of *chatHistory* is and render *chatItem* accordingly since Google might make changes.

Running our App

Let's run our app. I'll enter "Tell me about Taylor Swift" and press "Ask Me." It returns:

Can you tell me about...

user : tell me about taylor swift

model : **Taylor Alison Swift** (born December 13, 1989) is an American singer-songwriter. One of the most popular contemporary artists, she has sold over 200 million records worldwide, making her one of the best-selling music artists of all time. **Early Life and Career:** * Born in West Reading, Pennsylvania, Swift moved to Nashville at age 14 to pursue a country music career. * In 2006, she released her self-titled debut album, which became the best-selling country album of the year. * Swift's second album, "Fearless" (2008), was a critical and commercial success, winning multiple Grammy Awards and cementing her status as a country superstar. **Pop Transition:** * In the early 2010s, Swift began transitioning to pop music. * Her album "Red" (2012) featured both country and pop influences and solidified her crossover appeal. * "1989" (2014) marked Swift's full embrace of pop music and spawned some of her most iconic hits, including "Shake It Off" and "Blank Space." **Songwriting and Storytelling:** * Swift is known for her distinctive songwriting, which often explores themes of love, heartbreak, and personal growth. * Her songs are often highly personal and confessional, and she has been praised for her ability to connect with listeners on an emotional level. **Critical Acclaim and Awards:** * Swift has won numerous awards throughout her career, including 11 Grammy Awards, 34 American Music Awards, and 23 Billboard Music Awards. * She has been honored by Time magazine as one of the 100 most influential people in the world. **Personal Life and Philanthropy:** * Swift has been romantically linked to various celebrities, including Joe Jonas, Jake Gyllenhaal, and Harry Styles. * She is known for her charitable work and has donated millions of dollars to various causes, including disaster relief, education, and LGBTQ+ rights. **Current Work:** * Swift has released nine studio albums, the latest being "Midnights" (2022). * She is known for her elaborate and immersive live performances, and has embarked on several successful concert tours. * Swift has also ventured into acting, appearing in films such as "The Lorax" (2012) and "Cats" (2019). **Legacy:** Taylor Swift is a global pop icon who has transformed the music industry. Her groundbreaking songwriting, infectious melodies, and personal storytelling have resonated with millions of fans worldwide. She is widely regarded as one of the most influential and successful artists of her generation.

I can ask a follow-up question, leveraging the context of previous messages. For instance, "how old is she?"

By itself, we don't know who the 'she' is referring to. However, given the context, it's clear we're referring to Taylor Swift.

user : how old is she?

model : Taylor Swift is 33 years old. She was born on December 13, 1989.

This enables the continuation of a multi-chat conversation.

Improving the Chat UI

Let's improve the Chat UI a little. For each *chatItem*, we will use the React-Bootstrap's Toast component (react-bootstrap.netlify.app/docs/components/toasts):

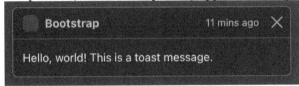

Make the changes in **bold**:

```
...
...
import Alert from 'react-bootstrap/Alert';
import Toast from 'react-bootstrap/Toast';
...
...
...

  return (
    <Container>
      ...
      ...
      {chatHistory.map((chatItem, _index) =>
        <Toast key={_index}>
          <Toast.Header closeButton={false}>
            <strong className="me-auto">{chatItem.role}</strong>
          </Toast.Header>
          <Toast.Body>{chatItem.parts[0].text}</Toast.Body>
        </Toast>
      )}
    </Container>
  );
```

Run the app again and our chat conversation now looks like:

Clear History

The final step is to clear the chat history, the input value, and any errors when necessary. Let's implement this functionality with a clear button. Upon clicking this button, we clear everything.

In the clear button, we add:

```
<Button variant="primary" type="submit" onClick={getResponse}>
  Ask Me
</Button>
<Button variant="secondary" type="submit" onClick={clear}>
  Clear
</Button>
```

Let's define this function by adding:

```
...
const clear = () => {
  setValue("")
  setError("")
  setChatHistory([])
}

return (
  <Container>
...
```

In it, we set *value* and *error* to be empty string and *chatHistory* to be an empty array again.

Here's the entire App.js (in case you missed anything):

```
import 'bootstrap/dist/css/bootstrap.min.css';
import Container from 'react-bootstrap/Container';
import Button from 'react-bootstrap/Button';
import Form from 'react-bootstrap/Form';
import {useState} from 'react';
import Alert from 'react-bootstrap/Alert';
import Toast from 'react-bootstrap/Toast';

function App() {
  const [error, setError] = useState("")
  const [value, setValue] = useState("")
  const [chatHistory, setChatHistory] = useState([])

  const getResponse = async() => {
    if (!value){
      setError("Please ask a question.")
      return
    }

    try{
      const options = {
        method: 'POST',
        body: JSON.stringify({
          history: chatHistory,
          message: value
        }),
        headers:{
          'Content-Type':'application/json'
        }
      }
      const response = await
fetch('http://localhost:8000/gemini',options)
      const data = await response.text()
      setChatHistory(oldChatHistory => [...oldChatHistory, {
        role:"user",
        parts:[{text:value}]
      },
        {
          role: "model",
          parts:[{text:data}]
        }
      ])
      setValue("")
      console.log(chatHistory)
    }
```

```
    catch(error){
      console.error(error)
      setError(error)
    }
  }

  const clear = () => {
    setValue("")
    setError("")
    setChatHistory([])
  }

  return (
    <Container>
        <Form.Control type="text" placeholder="Can you tell me about..."
                value={value}
                onChange={(e) => setValue(e.target.value)}
        />
        <Button variant="primary" type="submit" onClick={getResponse}>
          Ask Me
        </Button>
        <Button variant="secondary" type="submit" onClick={clear}>
          Clear
        </Button>
        {error &&
          <Alert key="danger" variant="danger">
            {error}
          </Alert>
        }
        {chatHistory.map((chatItem, _index) =>
          <Toast key={_index}>
            <Toast.Header closeButton={false}>
              <strong className="me-auto">{chatItem.role}</strong>
            </Toast.Header>
            <Toast.Body>{chatItem.parts[0].text}</Toast.Body>
          </Toast>
        )}
    </Container>
  );
}

export default App;
```

server.js code

And here's server.js (backend):

```
const PORT = 8000
const express = require('express')
const cors = require('cors')
const {GoogleGenerativeAI} = require("@google/generative-ai")
require('dotenv').config()
const app = express()
app.use(cors())
app.use(express.json())

const genAI = new GoogleGenerativeAI(process.env.API_KEY);

app.listen(PORT, () => console.log(`listening on port ${PORT}`))

app.post('/gemini', async (req, res) => {
    const model = genAI.getGenerativeModel({model:'gemini-pro'})
    const chat = model.startChat({
        history: req.body.history
    })

    const msg = req.body.message
    const result = await chat.sendMessage(msg)
    const response = await result.response
    const text = response.text()

    console.log(text)
    res.send(text)
})
```

Summary

Hopefully, you have enjoyed this book and would like to learn more from me. I would love to get your feedback, learning what you liked and didn't for us to improve.

Please feel free to email me at support@i-ducate.com if you encounter any errors with your code or to get updated versions of this book.

If you didn't like the book, or if you feel that I should have covered certain additional topics, please email us to let us know. This book can only get better thanks to readers like you. If you like the book, I would appreciate if you could leave us a review too. Thank you and all the best!

About the Author

Greg Lim is a technologist and author of several programming books. Greg has many years in teaching programming in tertiary institutions and he places special emphasis on learning by doing.

Contact Greg at support@i-ducate.com

www.ingramcontent.com/pod-product-compliance
Lightning Source LLC
LaVergne TN
LVHW081532050326
832903LV00025B/1758